The Power of
Prayer & Devotion

The Power of Prayer & Devotion
Copyright © 2024 by Yvonne Bronstorph

Published in the United States of America

Library of Congress Control Number: 2024902651

ISBN   Paperback: 979-8-89091-477-4
ISBN   eBook: 979-8-89091-478-1

All rights reserved. No part of this publication may be reproduced, stored in a retrieval system or transmitted in any way by any means, electronic, mechanical, photocopy, recording or otherwise without the prior permission of the author except as provided by USA copyright law.

The opinions expressed by the author are not necessarily those of ReadersMagnet, LLC.

ReadersMagnet, LLC
10620 Treena Street, Suite 230 | San Diego, California, 92131 USA
1.619. 354. 2643 | www.readersmagnet.com

Book design copyright © 2024 by ReadersMagnet, LLC. All rights reserved.

Cover design by Tifanny Curaza
Interior design by Don De Guzman

The Power of Prayer & Devotion

Scripture verses are from the New King James Version

Yvonne Bronstorph

Contents

Answered Prayers 1
Come Holy Spirit I Need You 3
In a Dry and Thirsty Land 5
In God We Must Trust 7
Look What the Lord Has Done 9
Removing the Mountains in Our Lives 11
Spirit of Fear 13
Striving For Holiness 15
The Gold Standard of God's Word 17
The Kingdom Within Us 19
The Lord is Our Shepherd 21
Victory Is Ours 23
Waiting on the Lord 25
Walking in Christ Means Sacrifice 27
What Is Life Without Thee 29
You Are Important 31
Your Human Worth and Divine Destiny 33

Answered Prayers

"Then He spoke the parable to them, that men always ought to pray and not lose heart."

Luke 18:1

In April 2000, I went into anaphylactic shock and was in the ICU. The doctors gave up on me, but my husband refused to accept their prognosis and called the pastor and church for prayer. The nurse came to insert a trachea tube in my throat as it was swelling and closing. I asked her to walk away for a few seconds, which she did. I lifted my voice to Jesus and said, "Please stop this swelling because I do not want this tube in my throat."

The nurse returned and examined my throat. She looked at me in disbelief and amazement and remarked, "I do not understand; your throat has no swelling." I believed in the power of prayer and divine healing. I just thanked Jesus for answering my prayer and am still thanking Him 21 years later.

Instead of accepting the doctors' prognosis, I called on the One who hears and answers prayers. Whose report do we believe? We believe the report of the Lord.

I submitted myself to the Lord in faith, trusting Him completely, knowing He is the Healer. Just as Jesus healed all who went to Him while He was on earth, He has never changed and continues to heal today.

When doctors gave up on me, God did not. He heard my cry and answered. Talk to God; tell Him the desires of your heart. In that moment of prayer when I called out to Jesus, there was such intimacy, with Him bringing an immediate answer. He hears. He knows. He understands.

"For I know the thoughts I think toward you, says the Lord, thoughts of peace and not evil, to give you a future and a hope. Then you will call upon Me and go and pray to Me, and I will listen."

Jeremiah 29:11

Come Holy Spirit I Need You

> "The Spirit Himself bears witness with our spirit that we are children of God."
>
> Romans 8:16

The promise gift of the Holy is personal, precious, present and permanent gift from the Father. When Jesus returned to His glory at the right hand of the Father in His infinite wisdom and benevolence sent the Holy Spirit to dwell in us. We therefore have in us a Comforter, Helper, Teacher, Advocate and guide. He is our best friend and by inviting Him into our everyday life and staying in step with Him we will be transformed us, both in our choices and relationships. In our live, at times we are at a place where we need someone to come in one of these capacities who else but the Holy Spirit. He wants to be activated in you.

The Holy Spirit is our anointing oil, live coal, bit and restrain leading us to live power, devotion, strength, and constrain. As our Teacher the Spirit will guide us in all truth as only He can give us the correct understanding of the truth of God's Word and reveal the deep things of God, as they are engraves on our hearts.

The indwelling work of the Holy Spirit enables us to strive to walk in the footsteps of Jesus and resist the enemy. Therefore yield to Him to work in you and grow spiritually in ways you cannot imagine possible because He knows the heart of God.

> "Likewise the Spirit also helps in our weaknesses. For we do not what we should pray for as we ought, but the Spirit Himself makes intercession for us with groaning which cannot be uttered".
>
> Romans 8:26

In a Dry and Thirsty Land

"O God, You are my God; early will I seek You; my soul thirsts for You; my flesh longs for You in a dry and thirsty land where there is no water."

Psalm 63:1

We are all living in a dry and thirsty land unless Jesus is the center of our lives. God, the Creator, Almighty One who spoke the heavens and the universe into existence, created the plants, animals, seas, oceans, mountains, and rivers is being forced into the past. God who created man in His own image longs for us to draw close to Him.

The world is in chaos. Moral values are rapidly disappearing, but worst of all people are without hope. They have put their hope in money, which is losing its value, drugs and alcohol to make them feel good and forget the pain, and other carnal evils to try and satisfy their desires.

We are spirit beings made in God's image and can never find peace and satisfaction in our souls as long as we are separated from God. Our spirit has to be in communion with the Father's spirit. When we make Jesus the Lord of our lives, we have hope of eternity with him. Our Christian walk is a pilgrimage, heaven our destination. Life on earth is just a minute compared to eternal life with Jesus.

Trust in Jesus and your thirst will be quenched by his river of living waters, flowing from the throne of the sovereign God in you. Life will be brimming with hope, peace, and joy.

"For I will pour water upon him who is thirsty, and floods on the dry ground; I will pour My Spirit on your descendants, and My blessing on your offspring."

Isaiah 44:3

In God We Must Trust

> "But let him ask in faith with no doubting for he who doubts is like a wave of the sea tossed by the wind."
>
> James 1:6

So often we doubt the promises of God in His Word. We struggle with thoughts of fear for our sons and daughters, who have gone the way of the prodigal son, and are swallowed up by the carnality of our world. They are attracted to the dangers of the secular world like a moth to a flame, and it is only a matter of time that they, like the moth, will go too near and be burnt or worse. Many nights we lie in our beds, praying and crying for them to look to God for their salvation.

We bring them before the Lord, standing on His promises, knowing that He loves them more than we can ever love them. We ask God to take their minds captive, that whatever is attracting them will become bitter tasting to their mouths and like red hot irons to their eyes. Command the enemy to take his hands off our children. Declare that they belong to God and are trophies of His grace.

God hears the cries of mothers' hearts and feels our pain. Prayerfully bring your children the altar, remembering that with God, all things are possible. The seeds that were sown in childhood may be covered with weeds and briars, but one day those seeds will spring up and begin to flourish. Do not doubt the power of prayer and stand firm of the promises of the sovereign God.

> "Refrain your voice from weeping, and your eyes from tears; For your work shall be rewarded says the Lord, and they shall come back from the land of the enemy. There is hope in your future says the Lord, that your children shall come back to their own border."
>
> Jeremiah 31:16

Look What the Lord Has Done

"Fear not, for I am with you; Be not dismayed, for I am your God. I will strengthen you, yes, I will help you, I will hold you up with My righteous right hand."

Isaiah 41:10

We get caught up in the mundane things in our lives and often run to God only when in a desperate situation. Every morning we wake, our first words should be, "Thank you Lord for another day."

He gave us another day to worship and glorify Him. Look around at His creation, the sun, flowers, trees, moon, seasons, but look at yourself and how much He loves you. He loves and cares for us so much that Jesus came and died a torturous death for our sins so we would live in eternity with Him. How often He healed us when we were sick and we did not know sickness, or protected us from danger when we did not see it. How often He carried us when the road was so rough we could not take another step, or filled us with peace when our world was falling apart.

Remember the job we so desperately wanted and got because a door that was closed opened, buying the house we dreamed about but thought impossible, a prodigal child's return home, and broken relationships mended. This is what the Lord has done for us.

Each day, let us be thankful for all we have rather than complain about the things we perceive we lack. Think of all the blessings because we can never list all the good things the Lord has done for us.

"Blessed be the God and Father of our Lord Jesus Christ, who has blessed us with every spiritual blessing in the heavenly places in Christ."

Ephesians 1:3

Removing the Mountains in Our Lives

> "So Jesus said to them, 'Because of your unbelief; for assuredly, I say to you, if you have the faith of a mustard seed, you will say to this mountain, move from here to there, and it will move; and nothing will be impossible for you.'"
>
> Matthew 17:20

What are the mountains in your life? Are they rejection, loneliness, illness, broken relationships, depression, and some form of addiction? We may ask the question: what can I do? The answer is, "Give it to Jesus who teaches that faith can move mountains."

We are created with a measure of faith, which comes alive and grows, as we mature spiritually by reading and meditating on the Word of God daily. We must learn to apply our faith to see those mountains move. One might ask, "How do I apply my faith?" This little faith, the size of a mustard seed, can grow into such faith in the Lord and His promises that it becomes a powerful weapon against the enemy, who comes only to kill, steal, and destroy.

Put your faith into acts of love and watch it grow. Speaking to the mountains in our lives is an act of faith which helps us grow in godly strength. Seeing those mountains removed by God's merciful hand encourages us to continue to believe in the miraculous. Remember our God is a miracle worker, the One who can do the impossible and reverse the irreversible. We serve a supernatural God.

> "For as the body without spirit is dead, so faith without works is dead also."
>
> James 2:26

Spirit of Fear

"For God has not given us a spirit of fear, but of power and love and a sound mind."
2 Timothy 1:17

When faced with devastating news or dire situations, we instantly develop a spirit of fear, which is a natural human reaction. We seem paralyzed and tormented, leading us to feel powerless and alone. Fear is not from our loving Father God.

This feeling of fear leads us to make wrong decisions and choices. We have within us the power of God through the Holy Spirit to be conquerors and not victims. God wants to pour His perfect love and His divine presence into our lives, which will help us make choices according to His will.

If we apply the truths taught by the word of God to our lives, then we will overcome fear and not be consumed by fear.

A relative of mine had a stroke and lost his ability to speak. One day, he communicated to me that he is often overcome by fear. I told him that whenever he feels that fear building up, "Call out in your mind the name of Jesus, He will still your fear as He did the storm." After that, I could see him relaxing and the fear disappear from his eyes.

" For the weapons of our warfare are not carnal but mighty in God for pulling down strongholds, casting down arguments and every high thing that exalts itself against the knowledge of God, bringing every thought into captivity to the obedience of Christ."
2 Timothy 10:4-5

Striving For Holiness

"Finally brethren, whatsoever things are true, whatsoever things are honest, whatsoever things are just, whatsoever things are pure, whatsoever things are of good report; if there be any virtue, and if there be any praise, think on these things."
                                          Philippians 4:8

When we strive to live a life walking in the footsteps of Jesus, we know that we will not be perfect. Instead, our pursuit should be the desire to be liberated from the things of the world that will restrict us from enjoying an effective power-filled life through the indwelling of the Holy Spirit. Remember the world is the enemy's playground and he is constantly dangling lies before our faces in an effort to confuse us and draw our attention away from God.

Sometimes, striving to walk the narrow path, we will lose friends and even family members who cannot accept the new person we have become in Jesus. The new creation we are will be attracted to life of praise and worship, have the loving heart of Jesus that reaches out to the lost and less fortunate, and wanting to spend time alone with Him.

The word of God is like a mirror that makes it possible for us to examine ourselves, so that we can see ourselves as God sees us. It cleanses, purges, guides, and directs, so that we can look at the changes we need to make, so we can strive to live holy as unto God. This world is not our home; we have an eternal home awaiting us.

"Just as He chose us in Him, before the foundation of the world, we should be holy and without blame before Him in love, having predestined us to adoption as sons by Christ Jesus to Himself, according to the good pleasure of His will."
                                          Ephesians 1:4-5

The Gold Standard of God's Word

> "Heaven and earth will pass away, but My Words will by no means pass away."
> Matthew 24:35

We hear about "gold standard" in the financial world and its importance in the economy. The only gold standard that should be important to us is the gold standard of God's Word. The Word of God has been given to us to set the spiritual and ethical standards by which we should live in order to enjoy an abundant life. His words will guide us as we live from day to day because they are the absolute, inerrant truth. They are sweeter than honey and music to our ears. They breathe life into our souls and refresh our spirit. God's promises given in His word are nuggets of gold — a life-line — as we navigate a world full of challenges, trials, and burdens. Whatever your circumstance or situation, there is a word of encouragement for a comparable story whether romance, intrigue, or mystery. These stories are as relevant today as they were many years ago.

The Word of God will open your eyes to the beauty of His character. They will soothe, comfort, strengthen, give peace and joy. Do not let anything rob you of the "joy of the Lord."

> "And I have put my words in thy mouth; and I have covered thee in the shadow of Mine hand, that I may plant the heavens, lay the foundation of the earth, and say unto Zion, 'You are My people.'"
> Isaiah 51:16

The Kingdom Within Us

> "The thief cometh not, but to steal, and to kill, and destroy; I am come that they may have life, and that they may have it abundantly."
>
> John 10:10

The economy is dissolving around us; countries are going bankrupt and the financial wizards cannot find solutions to the myriad of problems. We are working harder and earning less while IRA's and other retirement safety nets are decreasing in value. All the alarm bells are going off in our heads. Pause! Tell it to Jesus. Who is our only source? God. He owns everything we possess.

God is in control and has blessed us with all we have. He will strengthen us in times of plenty and times of scarcity as He provided for His people in Israel in the desert for forty years. He gave them manna and quail to eat; their clothes and shoes never wore out.

In the story of Joseph, God used him to save Egypt through seven years of famine. God, through Joseph, guaranteed the survival of the Hebrew people through whose ancestry Jesus was born.

Values change and earthy goods are fickle, but God and His promises never change. He is Jehovah Jireh, our Provider. Thank Him each day for all our possessions and even those we think we are lacking. We have to trust Him and Him only. Just as He provided for His people Israel, He will provide for us.

> "For godliness with contentment is great gain. For we brought nothing into this world, and it is certain we can carry nothing out. And having food and clothing, with these we shall be content."
>
> 1 Timothy 6:6-8

The Lord is Our Shepherd

"The Lord is my Shepherd; I shall not want. He makes me to lay down in green pastures ……"
                                                    Psalm 23:1

This is a psalm that we often pray and read, but do we really know our Shepherd? Jesus is the shepherd who tends His flock lovingly and protectively, ever watching over us with loving tender care. Just as the shepherd looks for the one lost sheep, in the same way, Jesus is seeking to draw us ever closer to Himself. Our Shepherd loves us so much that He died for us. He allowed His precious blood to be poured out at Calvary to be the atonement for our sins.

Just as the sheep are dependent on the shepherd for provision, guidance, and protection, so, too, are we dependent on Jesus — we are dependent on the Good Shepherd. Our Shepherd knows the "green pastures" and the "quiet waters" that will restore us. Only by following Him will we reach those places .

When we walk through "death's dark valley" our Shepherd, the Lord of life, is the only one who can ring us safely into the light.

He shall feed His flock like a shepherd; He shall gather the lambs with His arm, and carry them in His bosom, and shall gently lead those that are young."
                                                    Isaiah 40:11

Victory Is Ours

"But thanks be to God, who gave us the victory through our Lord Jesus Christ."

1 Corinthians 15:57

We are living in a time as never before! A pandemic has struck the world! Jobs and homes are being lost! The news from the doctor is not good! The world seems to be in chaos. Do not panic! Look up! We have a sovereign God who is bigger than all these circumstances and mountains facing us. As children of the one true God, we live in victory, because our God is the one who can reverse the irreversible, and make the impossible possible. He knows our needs, desires, and circumstances; just trust Him with every part of your life. He will not give you more than you can handle.

Sit and talk to Him. Pour out your heart; He is waiting to hear from you. He can open doors no one else can and shut those doors that need to be closed. Quiet your thoughts to hear His voice. We have victory through the blood of Jesus and the Word of the Lord. We belong to a victorious army marching forward that will not retreat with the cross of Jesus before us.

"For whatever is born of God overcomes the world. And this is the victory that has overcome the world – our faith."

1 John 5:4

Waiting on the Lord

> "Wait on the Lord; be of good courage, and He shall strengthen your heart; wait, I say on the Lord!
> **Psalm 27:14**

Waiting on the Lord requires discipline. When we pray, so often we want an immediate answer. We even become impatient and try to dictate to God how our prayer should be answered. God always knows what is best for us because He can see the future; we cannot. So His answer can be yes, wait, or no. Even if we think we know what might seem to us to be the right answer today, God, being all-knowing, can see that the future consequences are not in our best interest. God always has a better plan anyway. I know it is difficult to discipline ourselves to wait on God when our back is against a wall.

As we learn to wait, there is, fostered in us, a sensitivity of both His presence and love which quiets our hearts, and focuses our thoughts on Him. This awakens in us the desire to praise, worship, and give thanks. This allows Him to reveal to us in a gentle way any attitude or forgotten sins that would hamper our awareness of His voice.

Therefore, when you bring your requests to the Lord, leave them at the altar, meditate on is words and promises, focus on worship and praise. Spend time alone with Him, just waiting and allowing your spirit to connect with His spirit.

> "But they that wait on the Lord shall renew their strength; they shall mount up with wings as eagles; they shall run and not be weary; they shall walk and not faint."
> **Isaiah 40:31**

Walking in Christ Means Sacrifice

"I beech you therefore, brethren, by the mercies of God, that you present your bodies, a living sacrifice, holy, acceptable to God, which is your reasonable service."
Romans 12:1

When we strive to grow in the likeness of Christ or walk in His footsteps, it means we are willing to lay down our lives and take up the cross daily. On a regular basis, we will be confronted with our flesh, human desires, will and lusts, fighting against our spirit to control our lives. Jesus sacrificed His life so that we could enjoy an abundant spiritual life through His grace and mercy, and He invites us to resist the call of the carnal world in which we live. His death achieved what we could never achieve for ourselves, dragging us out of the depth of sin, and giving us eternal life with Him in glory.

When we take up our cross and bear it daily, it allows Him to reveal more of His glory and His will in our lives. We can then discover new dimensions of His unconditional love and in us, there will unfold a freedom to submit to His will for our lives.

Being Christ-like means we walk in humility in our service both to God and man. Jesus stepped down from His glory, humbling Himself to serve mankind, teaching us to love and serve each other.

We witnessed the gracious servant spirit of the sovereign God on earth.

"Therefore, if anyone is in Christ, he is a new creation; old things are passed away, behold, all things have become new."
2 Corinthians 5:17

What Is Life Without Thee

> "I will thee, O Lord, my strength. The Lord is my rock, and my fortress, and my deliverer; my God, my strength in whom I trust; my shield, and the horn of my salvation, and my high tower."
>
> Psalm 18:1-2

We must live with the Lord as the center of our lives. Without His hand to lead, guide, and direct us, our lives are like ships tossed in a storm, heading for the rocks or an airplane without a pilot. Unless we call on the Holy Spirit to be our pilot, the world around us will seem so attractive that that we will follow a path that leads to destruction. Our lives will seem unfulfilled because we are seeking purpose that can only come from a relationship with Jesus Christ.

Friend! Your world will fall apart if Jesus is not the center and guiding force. In Jesus is the hope of glory and fullness of life. God wants His love to flow from His throne — a love that is so deep, so strong, so wide, that it wraps itself around us and the impossible can become possible. We will experience peace beyond our understanding — a joy that wells up in us and flows to others and love without bounds. The Holy Spirit is waiting to be stirred up in us that we can live the abundant life Jesus bought for us with His blood.

> "The Lord is near to those who have a broken heart, and saves such as have a contrite spirit."
>
> Psalm 18:10

You Are Important

> "But God has chosen the foolish things of the word to put to sham the wise, and God has chosen the weak things of the world to put to shame the things that are mighty."
>
> 1 Corinthians 1:27

If you are feeling unappreciated, ignored, overlooked, and abused, remember God has a plan for your life and can use you for His glory. He uses the weak and ordinary to do His work. He used an eighty-year-old man to free a nation from slavery, a boy with a slingshot to defeat a giant, and a little boy's lunch to feed thousands. Jesus chose simple fishermen to be His disciples.

God created us all equal and we are all equally important to Him. God can use whom He desires as long as we are willing to be used by Him, whether you are a teacher, janitor, executive, or a homeless person. You may see yourself as insignificant yet God can rise you up in a mighty way to further His kingdom.

Everything created by God is significant because when we are weak, He is our strength. We are children of the one true living God, created in His image to praise and worship Him. You are valuable to your heavenly Father.

> "Fear not, for I am with you; be not dismayed; for I am your God; I will strengthen you; yes, I will help you, I will hold you up with My righteous right hand."
>
> Isaiah 41:10

Your Human Worth and Divine Destiny

> "What is man that You are mindful of him, and the son of man that You visit him? For You have made him a little lower than angels, and You have crowned him with glory and honor. You have made him to have dominion over the works of Your hand, You have put all things under his feet".
>
> Psalm 8:4-6

Man is distinct from all other creation because we are created in the likeness of God. As spirit beings made up of body, soul, and spirit, we are connected to God in a way no other creation is. As moral beings, our intellect, perception, and self-determination far exceed that of any other earthly creation. These character traits and our position of prominence in the order of creation imply our innate worth in the family of man as well as our individual value as children of God.

We should never be content to lie at a level of life below that which God destined us to live. We should strive to live life to the highest and fullest degree in spiritual abundance. If we live any other way, we are not being good stewards of the precious life entrusted to us by God. We have a responsibility that the rest of creation does not. Furthermore, we hold a critical role in the affairs of the earth, as guardians of "Mother Nature," even though we were created for a more noble purpose.

> "For You formed my inward parts; You covered me in my mother's womb. I will praise You, for I am fearfully and wonderfully made; marvelous are your works, and that my soul knows very well."
>
> Psalm 139:13-14

www.ingramcontent.com/pod-product-compliance
Lightning Source LLC
LaVergne TN
LVHW051922060526
838201LV00060B/4142